Modern and Classic Tractors Adult Coloring Book

Preston Guymon

ISBN-10: 1530178975
ISBN-13: 978-1530178971

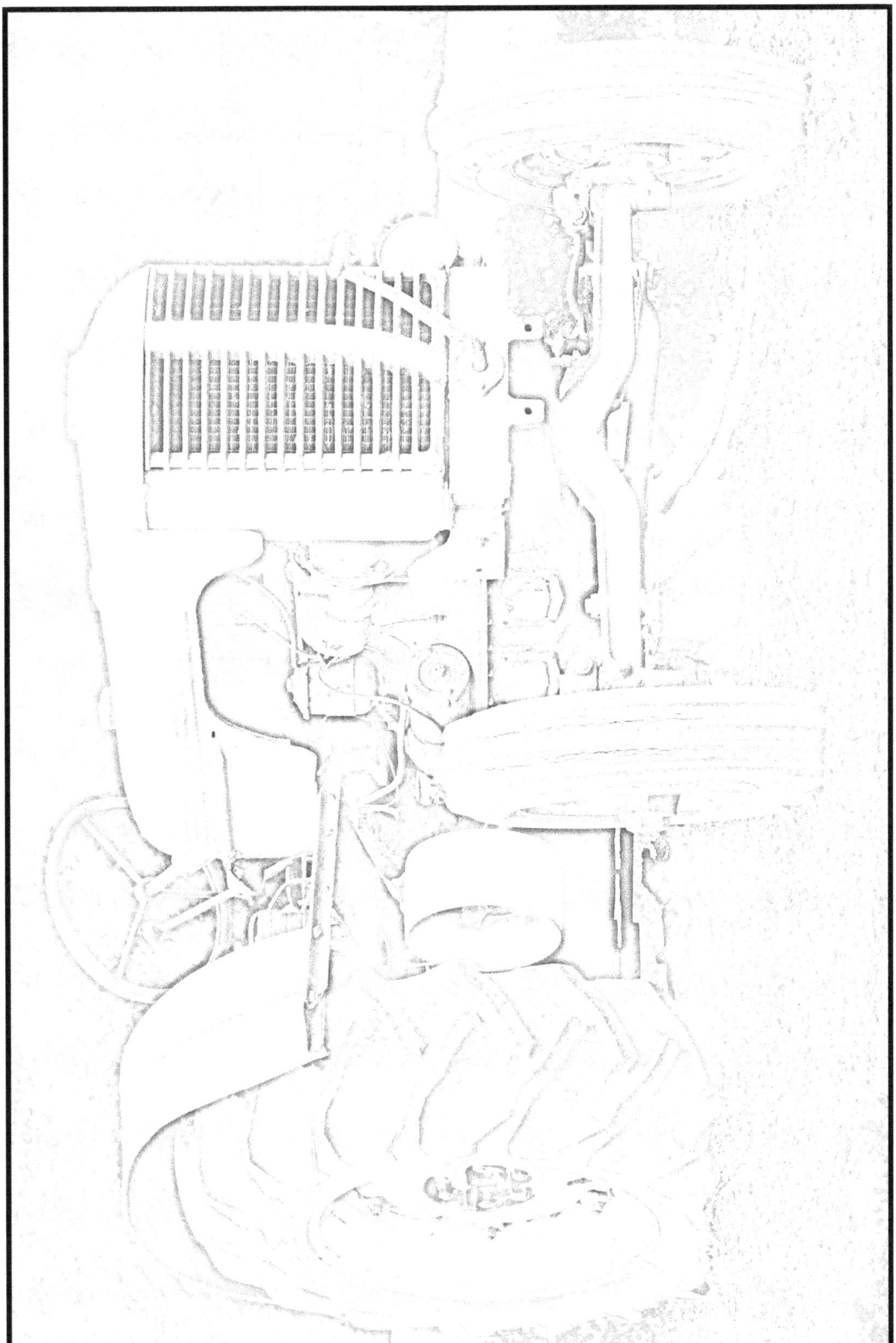

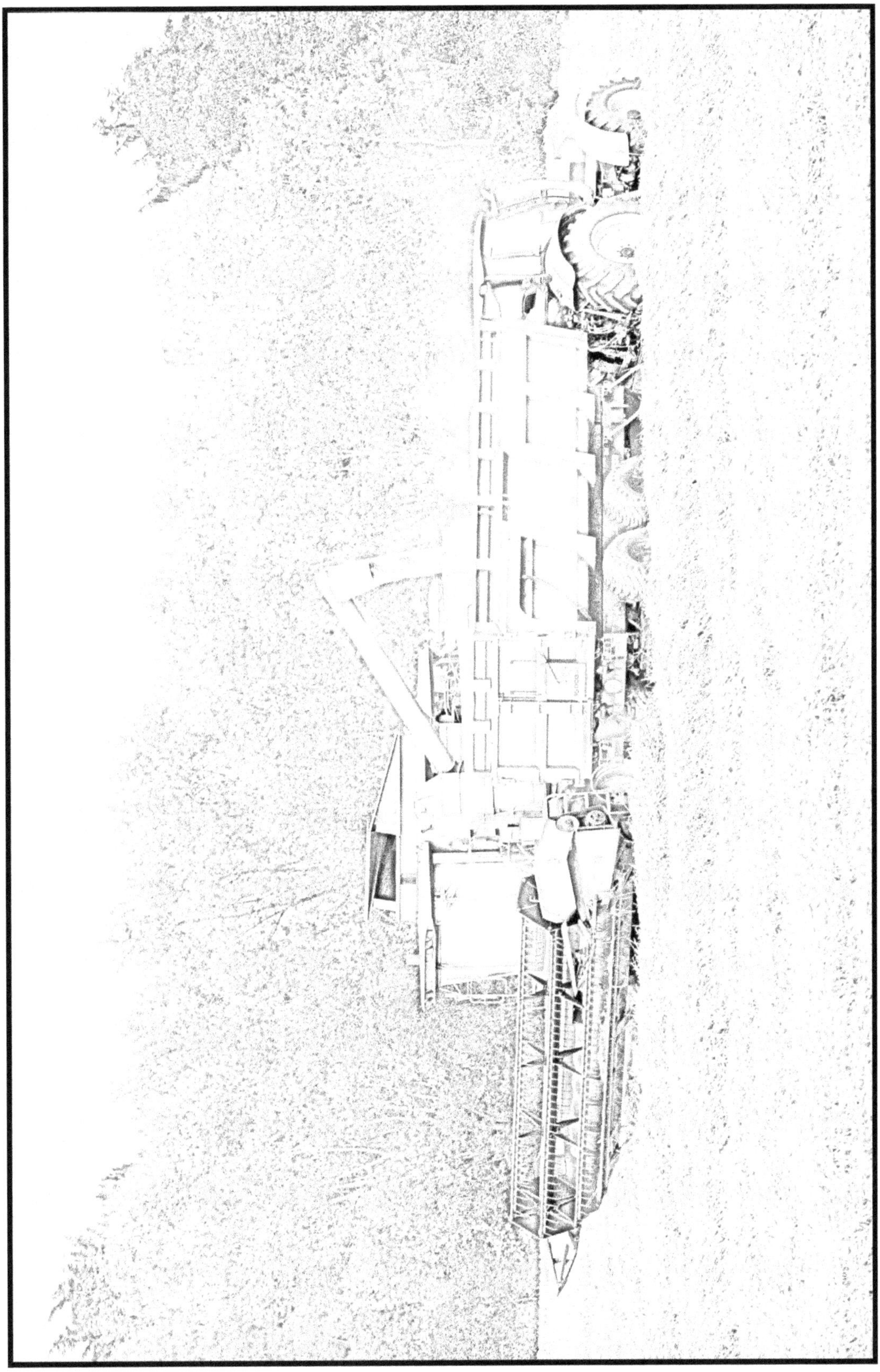

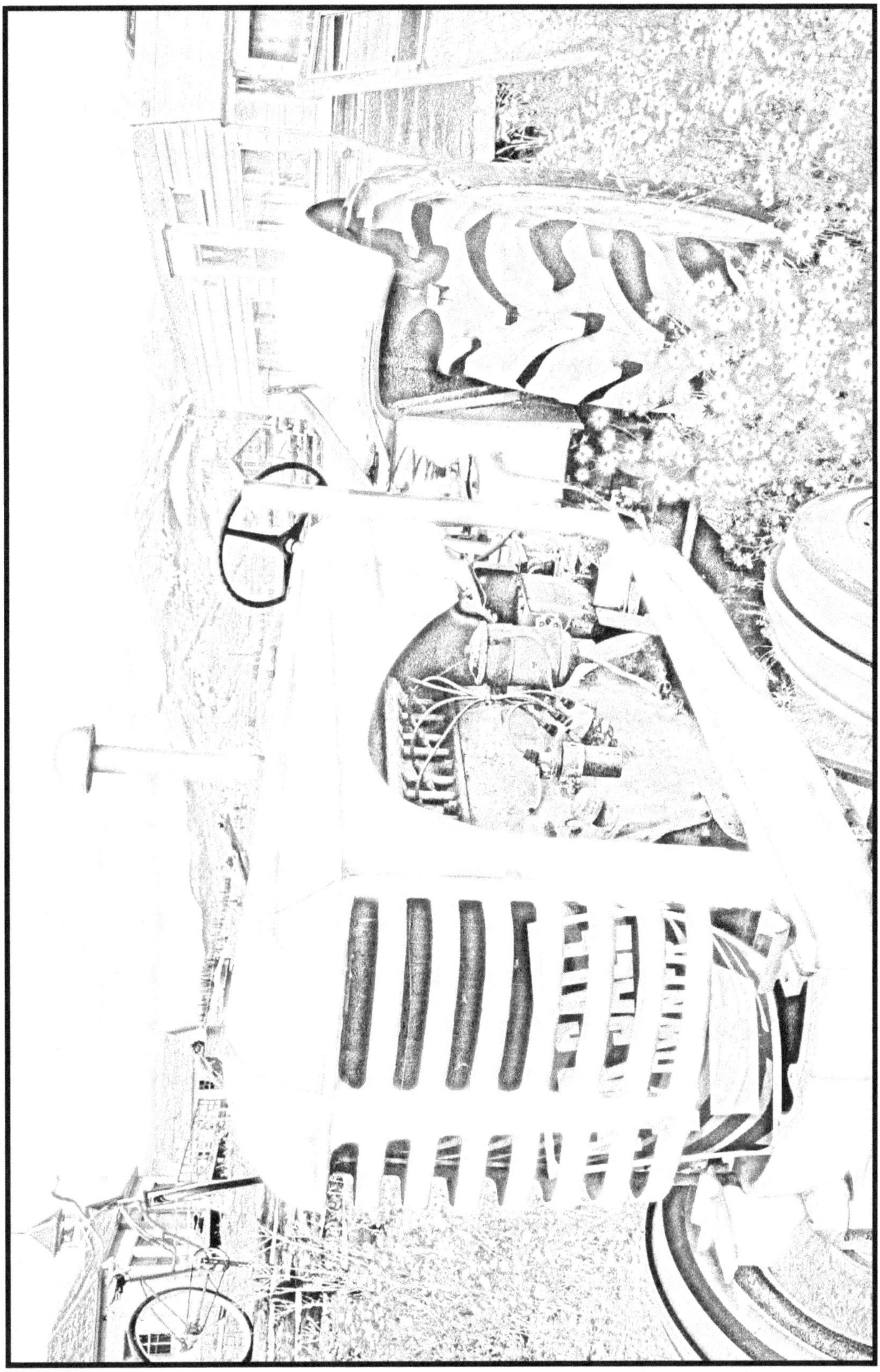

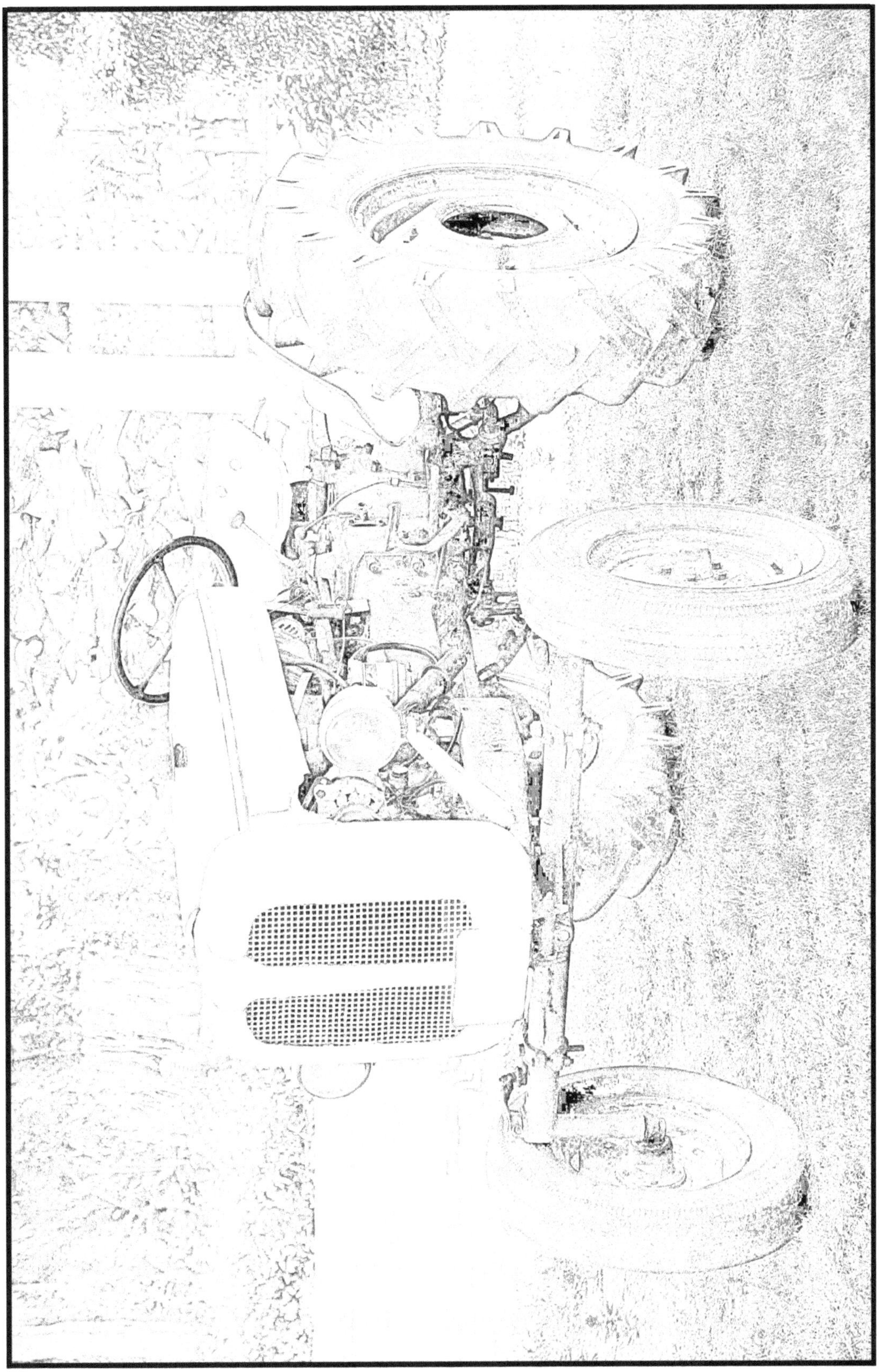

www.ingramcontent.com/pod-product-compliance
Lightning Source LLC
Chambersburg PA
CBHW081423280526
45788CB00009B/3211